Hal Leonard Student Piano Library

Piano Lessons

Book 5

FOREWORD

When music excites our interest and imagination, we eagerly put our hearts into learning it. The music in the **Hal Leonard Student Piano Library** encourages practice, progress, confidence, and best of all – success! Over 1,000 students and teachers in a nationwide test market responded with enthusiasm to the:

- variety of styles and moods
- natural rhythmic flow, singable melodies and lyrics
- "best ever" teacher accompaniments
- improvisations integrated throughout the **Lesson Books**
- orchestrated accompaniments included in audio and MIDI formats.

When new concepts have an immediate application to the music, the effort it takes to learn these skills seems worth it. Test market teachers and students were especially excited about the:

- "realistic" pacing that challenges without overwhelming
- clear and concise presentation of concepts that allows room for a teacher's individual approach
- uncluttered page layout that keeps the focus on the music.

The **Piano Practice Games** books are preparation activities to coordinate technique, concepts, and creativity with the actual music in **Piano Lessons**. In addition, the **Piano Theory Workbook** presents fun writing activities for review, and the **Piano Solos** series reinforces concepts with challenging performance repertoire.

The **Hal Leonard Student Piano Library** is the result of the efforts of many individuals. We extend our gratitude to all the teachers, students and colleagues who shared their energy and creative input. May this method guide your learning as you bring this music to life.

Best wishes,

Barbara Kreader   *Fred Kern*   *Phillip Keveren*

Authors
**Barbara Kreader, Fred Kern,
Phillip Keveren**

Consultants
Mona Rejino, Tony Caramia,
Bruce Berr, Richard Rejino

Editor
Carol Klose

Illustrator
Fred Bell

To access audio, visit:
www.halleonard.com/mylibrary
Enter Code
4143-6122-9551-1634

T0048544

ISBN 978-0-634-03122-9

HAL•LEONARD®

Copyright © 1998 by HAL LEONARD CORPORATION
International Copyright Secured   All Rights Reserved

Visit Hal Leonard Online at
www.halleonard.com

World headquarters, contact:
Hal Leonard
7777 West Bluemound Road
Milwaukee, WI 53213
Email: info@halleonard.com

In Europe, contact:
Hal Leonard Europe Limited
Dettingen Way
Bury St Edmunds, Suffolk, IP33 3YB
Email: info@halleonardeurope.com

In Australia, contact:
Hal Leonard Australia Pty. Ltd.
4 Lentara Court
Cheltenham, Victoria, 3192 Australia
Email: info@halleonard.com.au

REVIEW OF BOOK FOUR

NOTE AND REST VALUES

eighth rest
fills the time of
one eighth note

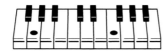

eighth note triplet
fills the time of
one quarter note

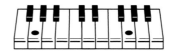

INTERVALS

Interval of a 7th

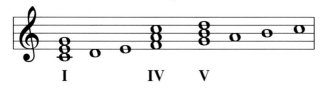

Interval of an Octave (8th)

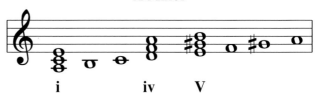

SCALES & PRIMARY TRIADS

C Major

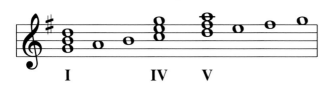

I   IV   V

A Minor

i   iv   V

G Major

I   IV   V

E Minor

i   iv   V

TIME SIGNATURES

3/8 (**3**) three beats fill every measure
eighth note gets one beat

6/8 (**6**) six beats fill every measure
eighth note gets one beat

common time **C** (**4**) another name for 4/4
has the feeling of four beats
per measure

cut time **₵** (**2**) two beats fill the measure
half note gets one beat

MUSICAL TERMS

accidentals – ♯, ♭, ♮ added to a piece outside
the key signature

allegretto **–** slightly slower than *allegro*

con moto **–** with motion

diminuendo (dim.) **–** gradually softer

dominant – 5th tone of the scale (V)

etude – exercise or study

giocoso **–** with humor

moderato **–** medium tempo

poco **–** a little; slightly

presto **–** very fast

sub-dominant – 4th tone of the scale (IV)

tenuto – give the note extra emphasis, holding it
for its full value

tonic – 1st tone of the scale (I)

vivace **–** lively

CONTENTS

PLAYING IN F MAJOR & D MINOR

Columns (right): Lesson Book | Theory Workbook | Solo Book

UNIT 1   EXPLORING SCALES

*✓

Title		Lesson Book	Theory Workbook	Solo Book
___ Windmill		4	3	3
___ The Bear		5		6
___ Arabesque		6	4	
___ Moving On Up	*F Major and D Minor*	8	6	
___ My Own Song	*improvising with motives and sequences*	10	8	
___ Spinning A Yarn		11	9	8
___ Wade In The Water		12		
___ Simple Gifts		13	11	10
___ Innocence		14		
___ A Minor Contribution		15		11

UNIT 2   DISCOVERING CHORDS

Title		Lesson Book	Theory Workbook	Solo Book
___ Cartoon Villain	*diminished and augmented triads*	16	12	
___ On The Rise	*primary and secondary triads*	17	13	
___ Curtain Call		18	16	12
___ The Clown	*open position triads in F Major*	20	17	14

PLAYING IN D MAJOR & B MINOR

UNIT 3   EXPLORING SCALES

Title		Lesson Book	Theory Workbook	Solo Book
___ Moving On Up	*D Major and B Minor*	22	18	19
___ My Own Song	*improvising question and answer phrases*	24	20	
___ A Whispered Promise		25	21	16
___ The Kind Cuckoo		26		
___ Nothing Could Be Finer Than Minor		27		18
___ Fantasia		28	23	20
___ Scherzino		29		22

UNIT 4   DISCOVERING CHORDS

Title		Lesson Book	Theory Workbook	Solo Book
___ Bouncing Back	*1st inversion triads*	30	24	24
___ Michael, Row The Boat Ashore	*2nd inversion triads*	31	25	27
___ Romance In B Minor		32		30
___ Bethena		34		32

PLAYING IN B♭ MAJOR & G MINOR

UNIT 5   EXPLORING SCALES

Title		Lesson Book	Theory Workbook	Solo Book
___ Moving On Up	*B♭ Major and G Minor*	36	28	29
___ My Own Song	*improvising in A B A form*	38	30	
___ Allegro		39		
___ Menuet In G Minor		40		35
___ Inspector Hound Returns	*chromatic scales*	42	31	38
___ Prelude		43	33	

UNIT 6   PUTTING IT ALL TOGETHER

Title		Lesson Book	Theory Workbook	Solo Book
___ Wanderer's Song			34	40
___ Everybody's Blues		46	35	42
___ German Dance		47	36	
___ Canon In D		48	37	44
___ Glossary, Master Composers		51	38	
___ Scales And Cadences	*keys: C, G, F, D, B♭ and Am, Em, Dm, Bm, Gm*	52		
___ Chords Of The Key	*root position, 1st and 2nd inversions; open positions*	54		
___ Certificate		56		

Students can check pieces as they play them.

Windmill

Wistfully (♩. = 86)  1/2

Phillip Keveren

*molto - much

The Bear

Vladimir Rebikoff
(1866-1920)

Andante pesante* (♩=90) **3/4**

*pesante - heavy

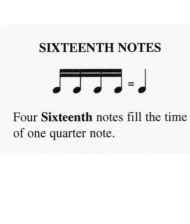

Arabesque

Fredrich Burgmüller
(1806-1874)
Op. 100

Allegro scherzando* (♩=110) 5/6

scherzando - playfully   *leggiero* - lightly   *sfz sforzando* - sudden strong accent

F Major Scale Pattern

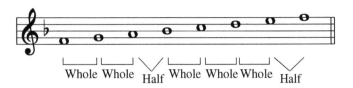

Whole Whole Half Whole Whole Whole Half

The Primary Triads in **F Major** are:

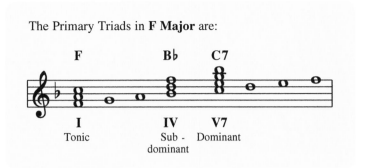

F	B♭	C7
I	IV	V7
Tonic	Sub-dominant	Dominant

Moving On Up

Key of F Major
Key signature: *one flat, B♭*

Moderato

Accompaniment (Student plays one octave higher than written.)

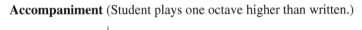 **8**

Moderato (♩=110)

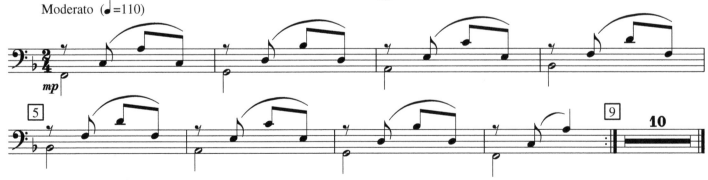

Extra for Experts
Turn to page 52 to play scales and cadences in **C Major** and **G Major**.

D Minor Scale Patterns

Natural Minor

The *Harmonic Minor Scale*
raises the seventh tone one half-step (C♯).

The Primary Triads in **D Minor** are:

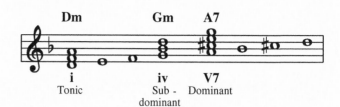

Dm	Gm	A7
i	iv	V7
Tonic	Sub - dominant	Dominant

Moving On Up

Key of D Minor
Key signature: *one flat, B♭*

First, play the *Natural Minor Scale* with the B♭ only.
On the repeat, play the *Harmonic Minor Scale* with the raised 7th (C♯).

Accompaniment (Student plays two octaves higher than written.) 🔊 **10**

First, play the natural form with the B♭ only. On the repeat, play the harmonic form with the raised 7th (C♯).

Extra for Experts
Turn to page 53 to play scales and cadences in **A Minor** and **E Minor**.

My Own Song
in F Major & D Minor
Improvising with Motives and Sequences

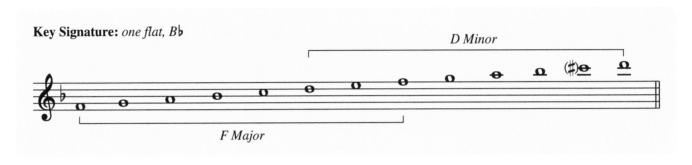

Key Signature: *one flat, B♭*

MOTIVE

A **Motive** is a short pattern of notes that reappears throughout a piece.

SEQUENCE

A **Sequence** is the repetition of the same pattern of notes (motive) at a different pitch.

Shape your improvisation using **motives** and **sequences**.

1. Play the following one-measure **motive**.
   Improvise by playing various **sequences** of this motive using notes from the F Major Scale.

2. Play the following one-measure **motive**.
   Improvise by playing various **sequences** of this motive using notes from the D Harmonic Minor Scale.

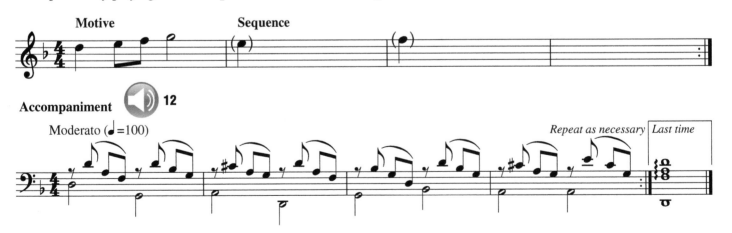

Extra for Experts

As you listen to the accompaniment in F Major, create your own motive and improvise various sequences.
Do the same in D Minor.

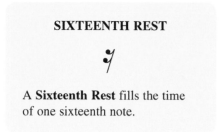

Spinning A Yarn

Phillip Keveren

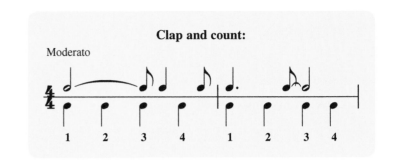

Wade In The Water

Spiritual
Arranged by Fred Kern

Moderato (♩=140) **15/16**

SIXTEENTH NOTE PATTERNS

Clap and count:

Simple Gifts

American
Arranged by Barbara Kreader

Flowing (♩=104)

Innocence

Fredrich Burgmüller
(1806-1874)
Op. 100

* *grazioso* - gracefully

A Minor Contribution

Chord Qualities

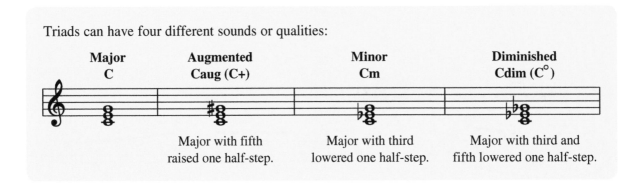

Triads can have four different sounds or qualities:

Major C	Augmented Caug (C+)	Minor Cm	Diminished Cdim (C°)
	Major with fifth raised one half-step.	Major with third lowered one half-step.	Major with third and fifth lowered one half-step.

Cartoon Villain

Slowly (♩=88) 24

Phillip Keveren

* accel. (accelerando) - becoming faster

Extra for Experts

Transpose *Cartoon Villain* to **G Major** and **F Major**.

Chords of the Key

PRIMARY TRIADS

Chords built on the 1st, 4th, and 5th tones of the major scale are called **Primary Triads**.

These triads are **major** and use *upper case* Roman Numerals **I - IV - V**.

SECONDARY TRIADS

Chords built on the 2nd, 3rd, and 6th tones of the major scale are called **Secondary Triads**.

These triads are **minor** and use *lower case* Roman Numerals **ii - iii - vi**.

On The Rise

The chord built on the 7th tone of the major scale is diminished (**vii°**).

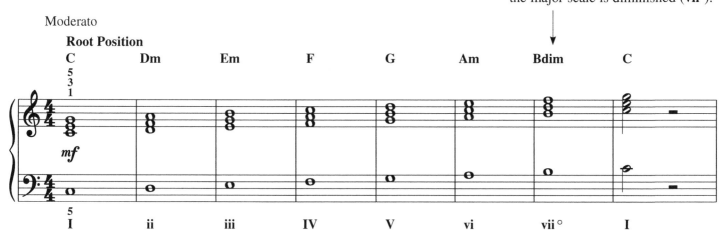

Open Position - one or more chord tones moved an octave higher or lower.
In these open chords, the 3rd is moved an octave higher.

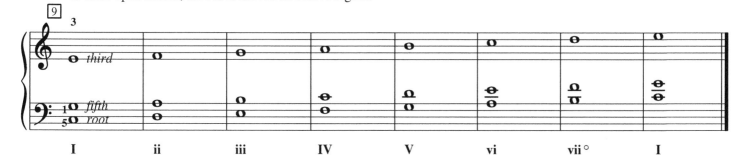

Accompaniment 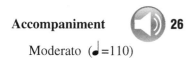 **26**

Extra for Experts
Turn to pages 54-55 to play Chords of the Key in **G Major** and **F Major** in root and open positions.

Curtain Call

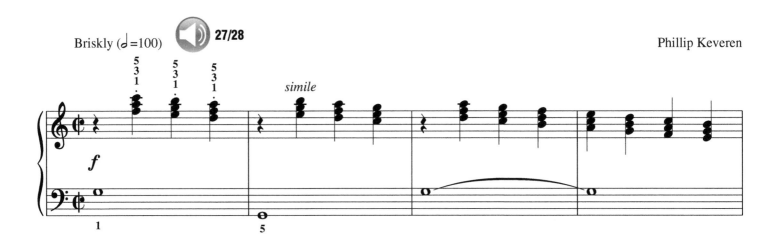

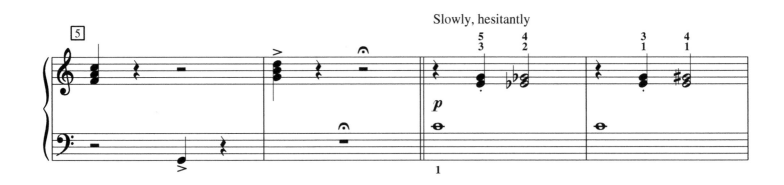

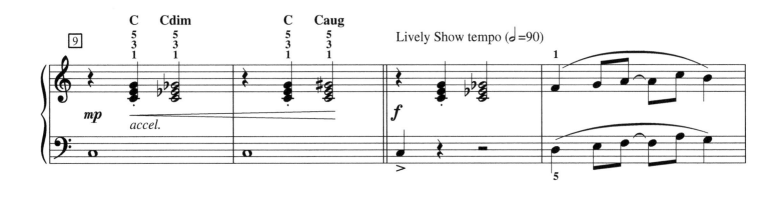

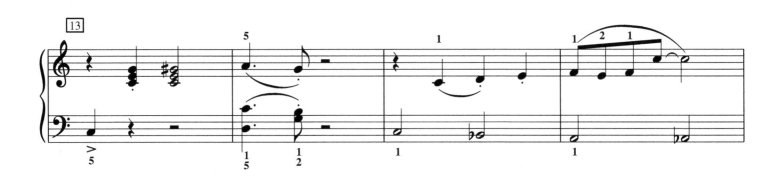

Open Position Triads in F Major:

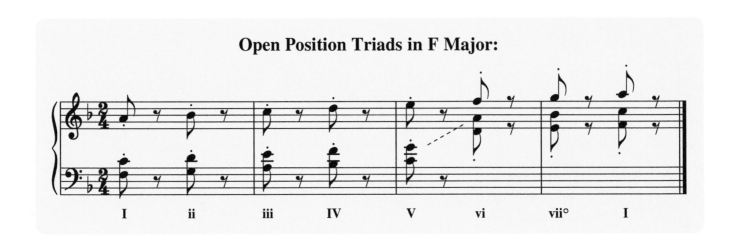

I   ii   iii   IV   V   vi   vii°   I

The Clown

Vladimir Rebikov
(1866 - 1920)

Allegretto (♩=96)   29/30

D Major Scale Pattern

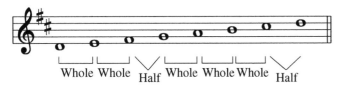

The Primary Triads in **D Major** are:

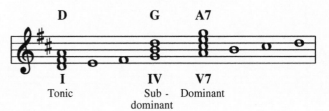

Moving On Up

Key of D Major
Key signature: *two sharps, F♯ C♯*

Moderato

Accompaniment (Student plays two octaves higher than written.)

Moderato (♩=110)

Extra for Experts
Turn to page 52 to play the scale and cadence in **F Major**.

B Minor Scale Patterns
Natural Minor

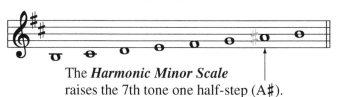

The *Harmonic Minor Scale* raises the 7th tone one half-step (A♯).

The Primary Triads in **B Minor** are:

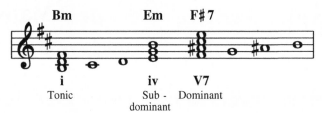

Bm	Em	F♯7
i	iv	V7
Tonic	Sub-dominant	Dominant

Moving On Up

Key of B Minor
Key signature: *two sharps, F♯ C♯*

First, play the *Natural Minor Scale* with the F♯, C♯ only.
On the repeat, play the *Harmonic Minor Scale* with the raised 7th (A♯).

Accompaniment (Student plays two octaves higher than written.) 🔊 34

First, play the natural form with the F♯, C♯ only. On the repeat, play the harmonic form with the raised 7th (A♯).

Extra for Experts

Turn to page 53 to play the scale and cadence in **D Minor.**

My Own Song
in D Major & B Minor
Improvising Question and Answer Phrases

Key Signature: *two sharps, F♯ C♯*

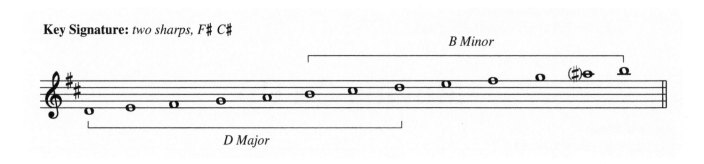

Shape your improvisation using **question** and **answer** phrases.

1. Play the following two-measure **question** phrase. Improvise various **answers** using notes from the D Major Scale.
    *   *Parallel answers* begin with the same pitches and include an almost identical ending.
    *   *Contrasting answers* include musical material different from the question.

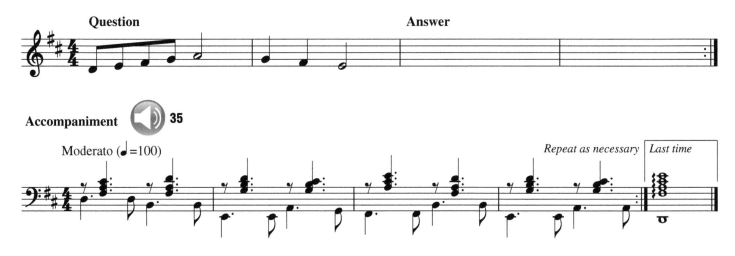

1. Play the following two-measure **question** phrase.
    Improvise various **answers** using notes from the B Harmonic Minor Scale.

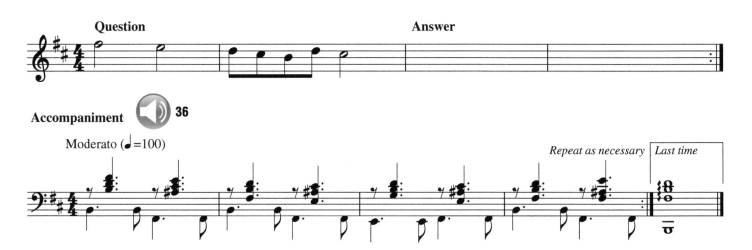

Extra for Experts
As you listen to the accompaniment in D Major, create your own question and improvise various answers.
Do the same in B Minor.

A Whispered Promise

Phillip Keveren

* dolce - sweetly

The Kind Cuckoo

Les Coucous Benevoles

François Couperin
(1668-1733)

Moderato (♩=90) 39/40

Nothing Could Be Finer Than Minor

Slowly (Four heavy beats to the measure) (♩=90) **41/42**

Bill Boyd

Fantasia

Georg Philipp Telemann
(1681-1767)

Scherzino

Samuel Maykapar
(1867-1938)

leggierissimo - very lightly   ***ppp*** - very, very softly

Chords of the Key

Root, First, and Second Inversions

A triad can have **three** positions:

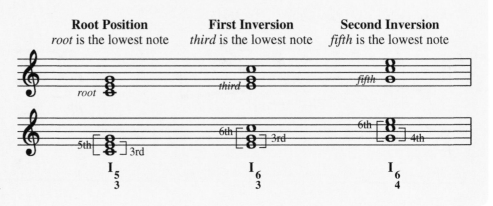

Roman numerals indicate each chord's root and its scale degree. When a chord is inverted, the lowest note changes but the letter names of the three chord tones remain the same. **Inversions** are identified by the chord tone that is the lowest note.

Chords of the Key in First Inversion

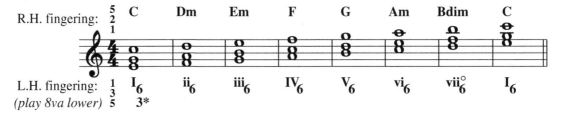

R.H. fingering: 5 2 1

| | C | Dm | Em | F | G | Am | Bdim | C |

L.H. fingering: 1 3 5
(play 8va lower)

I_6 ii_6 iii_6 IV_6 V_6 vi_6 vii°_6 I_6
3*

Bouncing Back

47/48

Tempo de dribble ($\quad$=170)

Phillip Keveren

* In **first inversion** chords, the number 3 indicating the interval of a 3rd is generally omitted, and the chord symbol is often abbreviated: I_6, ii_6, etc.

Chords of the Key in Second Inversion

Michael, Row The Boat Ashore

49/50

Simply and smoothly (♩=96)

American
Arranged by Fred Kern

Extra for Experts

Turn to page 54 to play Chords of the Key in **G Major**, **F Major**, and **D Major** in first and second inversions.

Romance In B Minor

Andante espressivo * (♩ = 112)

Phillip Keveren

* *espressivo* - expressively, emotionally

* *subito* - suddenly

Bethena

Scott Joplin
(1868-1917)
Arranged by Fred Kern

Waltz tempo (♩=108)   53/54

B♭ Major Scale Pattern

Whole Whole Half Whole Whole Whole Half

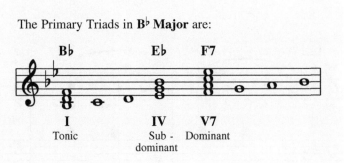

The Primary Triads in **B♭ Major** are:

B♭   E♭   F7

I   IV   V7

Tonic   Sub-   Dominant
        dominant

Moving On Up

Key of B♭ Major
Key signature: *two flats, B♭ E♭*

Accompaniment (Student plays two octaves higher than written.) 🔊 **56**

Extra for Experts
Turn to page 52 to play the scale and cadence in **D Major**.

G Minor Scale Patterns
Natural Minor

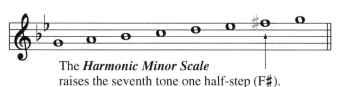

The *Harmonic Minor Scale*
raises the seventh tone one half-step (F♯).

The Primary Triads in **G Minor** are:

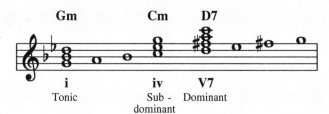

Gm	**Cm**	**D7**
i	**iv**	**V7**
Tonic	Sub - dominant	Dominant

Moving On Up

Key of G Minor
Key signature: *two flats, B♭ E♭*

First, play the *Natural Minor Scale* with the B♭, E♭ only.
On the repeat, play the *Harmonic Minor Scale* with the raised 7th (F♯).

Accompaniment (Student plays one octave higher than written.) **58**

First, play the natural form with the B♭, E♭ only. On the repeat, play the harmonic form with the raised 7th (F♯).

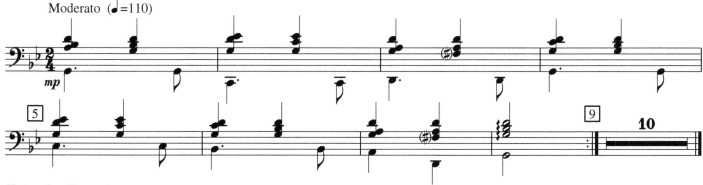

Extra for Experts
Turn to page 53 to play the scale and cadence in **B Minor**.

My Own Song
in B♭ Major & G Minor
Improvising in A B A Form

Key Signature: *two flats, B♭ E♭*

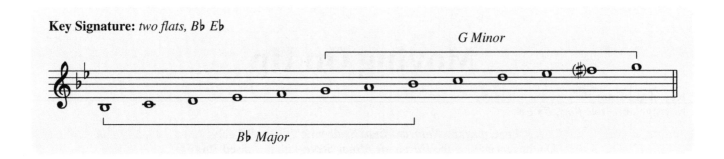

Shape your improvisation using **A B A form**.

1. To create the **A section**, play the following two-measure question phrase.
    Improvise various answers (*parallel* or *contrasting*), using notes from the B♭ Major Scale.

2. To create the **B section**, play the following motive. Improvise various sequences using notes from the
    G Harmonic Minor Scale.

Return to the **A section** in B♭ Major.

Accompaniment

Allegro

Allegro (♩=95) 60/61

Wolfgang Amadeus Mozart
(1756 - 1791)

Extra for Experts
Turn to page 52 to play the scale and cadence in **B♭ Major.**

Menuet In G Minor

From the *Notebook for Anna Magdalena Bach*

Allegro moderato (♩=100) **62/63**

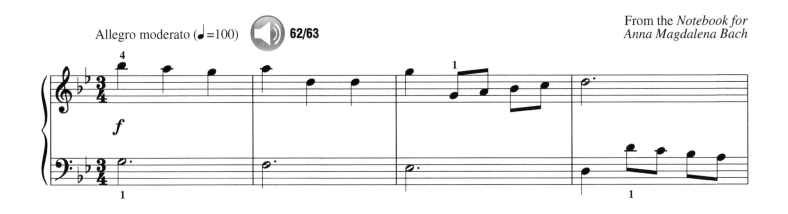

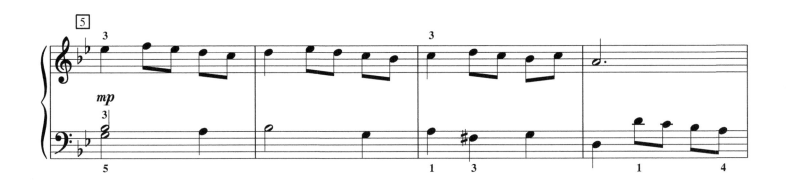

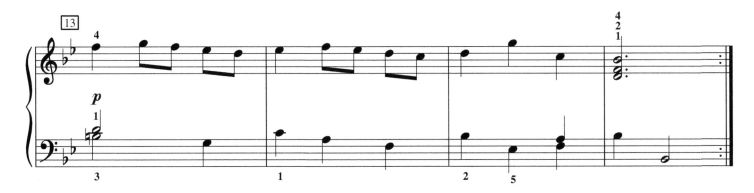

Extra for Experts

Turn to page 53 to play the scale and cadence in **G Minor.**

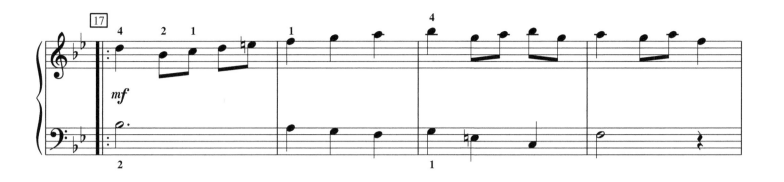

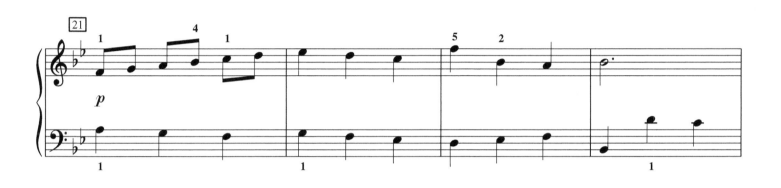

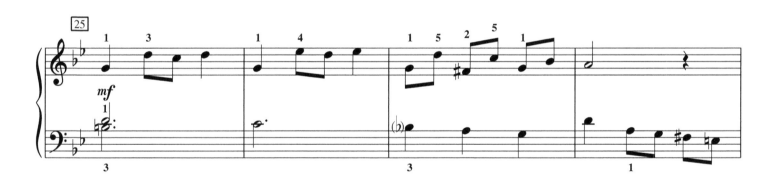

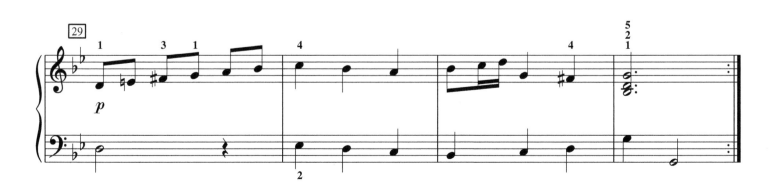

41

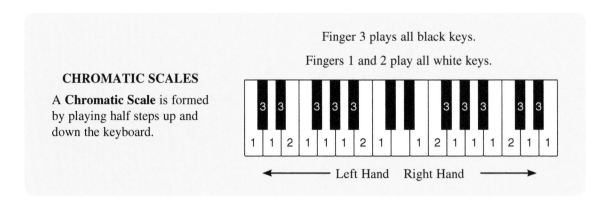

CHROMATIC SCALES

A **Chromatic Scale** is formed by playing half steps up and down the keyboard.

Finger 3 plays all black keys.

Fingers 1 and 2 play all white keys.

Left Hand   Right Hand

Inspector Hound Returns

Sneaky (♩=128)   **64/65**

Phillip Keveren

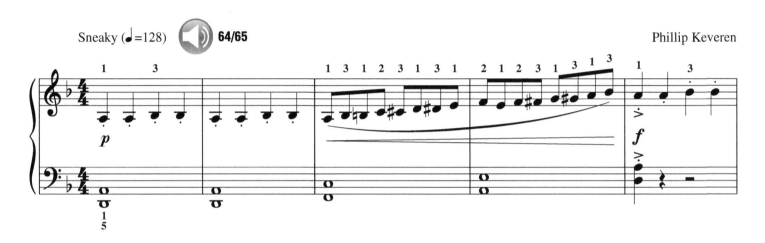

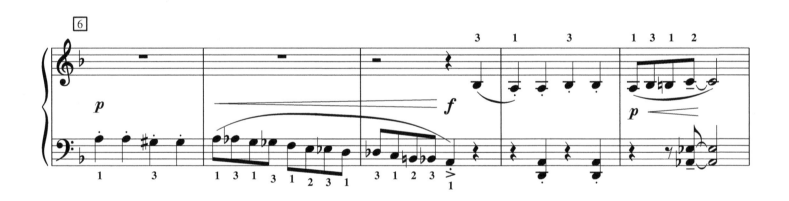

Prelude

Giuseppe Concone
(1801-1861)
Op. 37

* $\hat{\rho}$ - *sforzando accent*

Wanderer's Song

Hugo Reinhold
(1854-1935)

Allegretto (♩=96) 68/69

Extra for Experts

Turn to page 54 to play Chords of the Key in **B♭ Major,** in root, first, and second inversion.

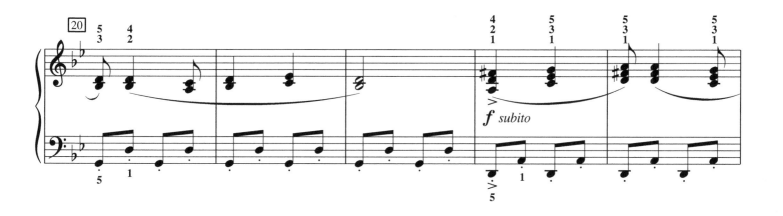

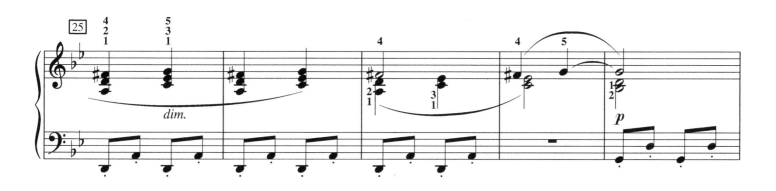

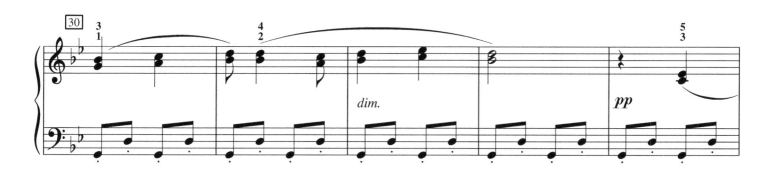

morendo - "dying;" fading away

Everybody's Blues

Swing (♪♪ = ♪³♪) (♩=120) **70/71**

Bill Boyd

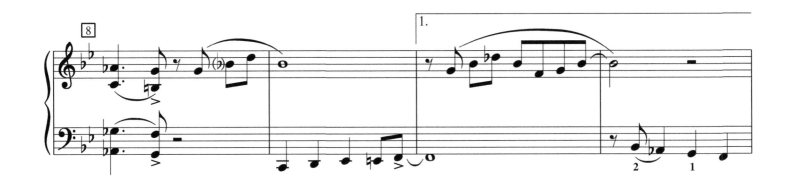

German Dance

Ludwig van Beethoven
(1770-1827)

Canon In D

Johann Pachelbel
(1653-1706)
Arranged by Fred Kern

* *allargando* - broad *ritard*

GLOSSARY

Accelerando	Becoming faster.	*Molto*	Very.
Allargando	Broad *ritard*.	**Motive**	A short pattern of notes that reappears throughout a piece.
Arabesque	A fanciful piano piece; "Arabian."		
Augmented triad	A Major triad with the fifth raised one half-step.	*Morendo*	"Dying;" fading away.
		Open position	Chord with one or more tones moved an octave higher or lower.
Canon	A melody that is repeated exactly by a different voice.	**Parallel answer**	A phrase that repeats its question note for note.
Chromatic	Moving by half-steps.	*Pesante*	Heavily.
Close position	Chord tones played as close together as possible, usually within an octave.	**Pitch**	The highness or lowness of a tone.
		Poco a poco	Little by little.
Contrasting answer	A phrase that begins the same as the question but varies the ending.	*Portato*	Half *staccato*; halfway between *staccato* and *legato*.
Diminished triad	A Minor triad with the fifth lowered one half-step.	*Portamento*	A smooth glide from one note to another.
Dolce	Sweetly.	**Primary triad**	Triad built on the 1st, 4th, or 5th tone of any scale.
Espressivo	Expressively, emotionally.		
Free-style answer	A phrase that is completely different from its question.	*Scherzando*	Playfully.
		Secondary triad	Triad built on the 2nd, 3rd, or 6th tone of any scale.
Grace note	An ornamental note, usually played quickly, before the beat.	**Sequence**	Repetition of the same pattern of notes at a different pitch.
Grazioso	Gracefully.	*Sforzando* *sfz*	A sudden strong accent.
Inversion	A chord in which the bass note is not the root.	*Sforzando accent*	
Key	The tonal center based on the tonic note of the scale.	*Subito*	Suddenly.
Leggiero	Lightly.	*Tempo primo*	Return to first tempo.
Marcato	Stressed, accented note.		
Menuet (Minuet)	A French dance from the mid-1600's in slow $\frac{3}{4}$ time.		

MASTER COMPOSERS IN PIANO LESSONS BOOK FIVE

Baroque
1600

Johann Pachelbel (1653-1706)
German baroque composer and organist.
Although he wrote several pieces for organ, his most
popular composition is the *Canon in D* for strings.

François Couperin (1668-1733)
French baroque composer.

Georg Philipp Telemann (1681-1767)
German baroque and pre-classical composer. He wrote much
sacred music as well as many operas, concertos, and sonatas.

Classical
1750

Wolfgang Amadeus Mozart (1756-1791)
Austrian classical composer.
He began writing music at the age of five.

Giuseppe Concone (1801-1861)
Italian classical composer.

Ludwig van Beethoven (1770-1827)
German composer and pianist whose style bridged the
classical and romantic eras. Among his many enduring
works are 9 symphonies, 32 piano sonatas, and 5
piano concertos. During his final years, he wrote many
compositions despite being completely deaf.

Romantic
1820

Fredrich Burgmüller (1806-1874)
German romantic composer who mainly composed study
pieces for piano.

Hugo Reinhold (1854-1935)
German romantic composer.

Vladimir Rebikov (1866-1920)
Russian contemporary composer.

Scott Joplin (1868-1917)
African-American popular composer,
known as the "King of Ragtime."

Samuel Maykapar (1867-1938)
Russian contemporary composer.

CONTEMPORARY
1900

Major Scales and Cadences

Play each scale:
- *Hands separately.*
- *Contrary Motion* – start on the same tonic note and play in opposite directions.
- *Parallel Motion* – play as written.

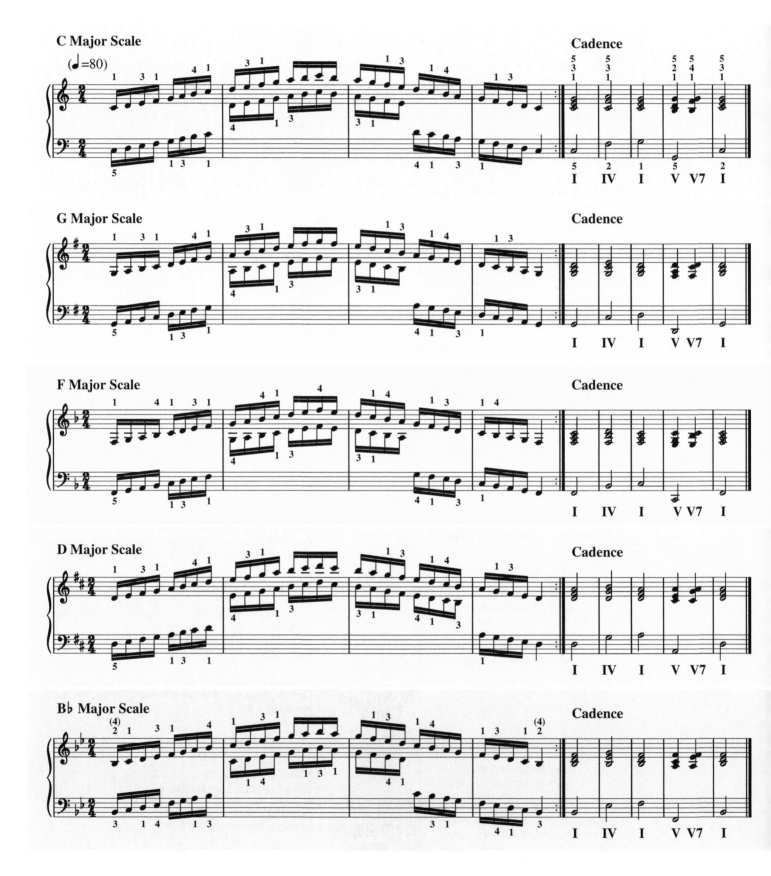

52

Minor Scales and Cadences

Play each **Harmonic Minor Scale:**
- *Hands separately.*
- *Contrary Motion* – start on the same tonic note and play in opposite directions.
- *Parallel Motion* – play as written.

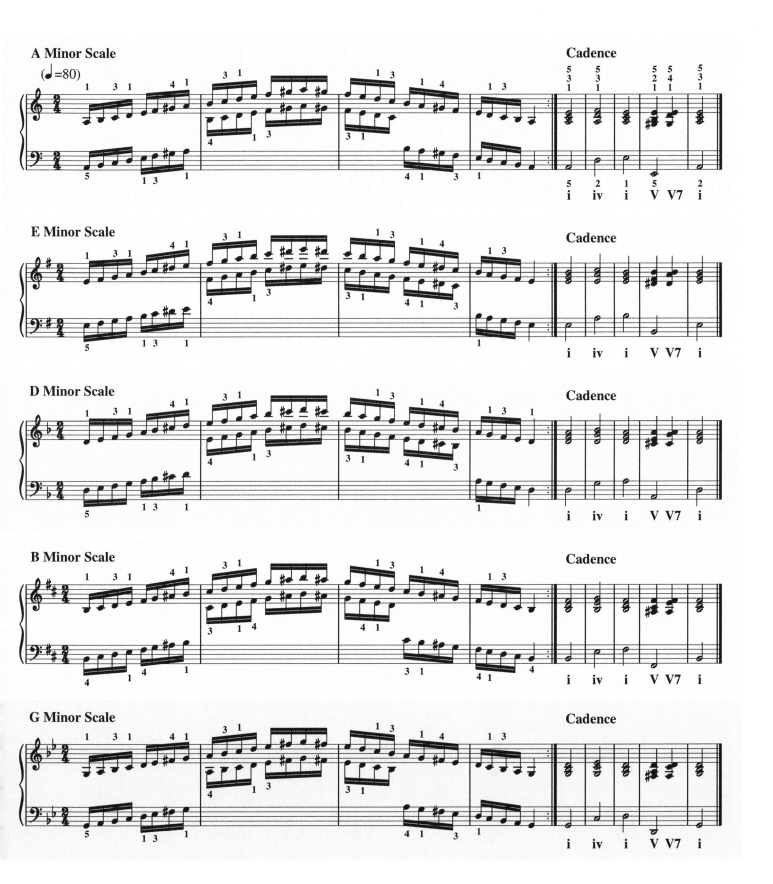

Chords of the Key
Root Position & Inversions

Observe the following chord fingering for each hand:

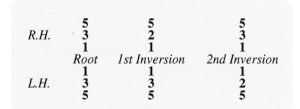

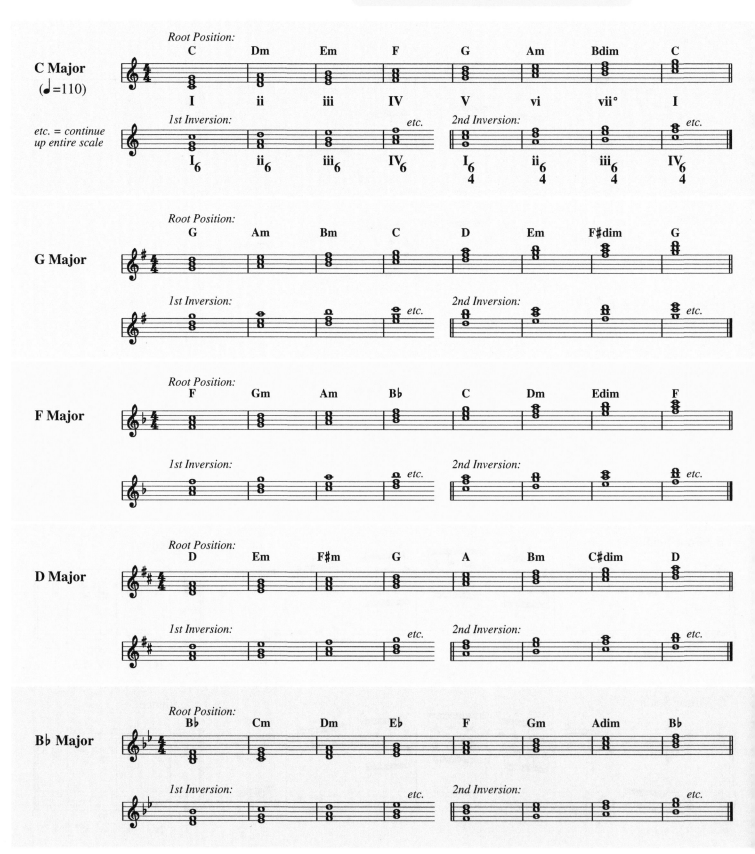

Chords of the Key
Open Position

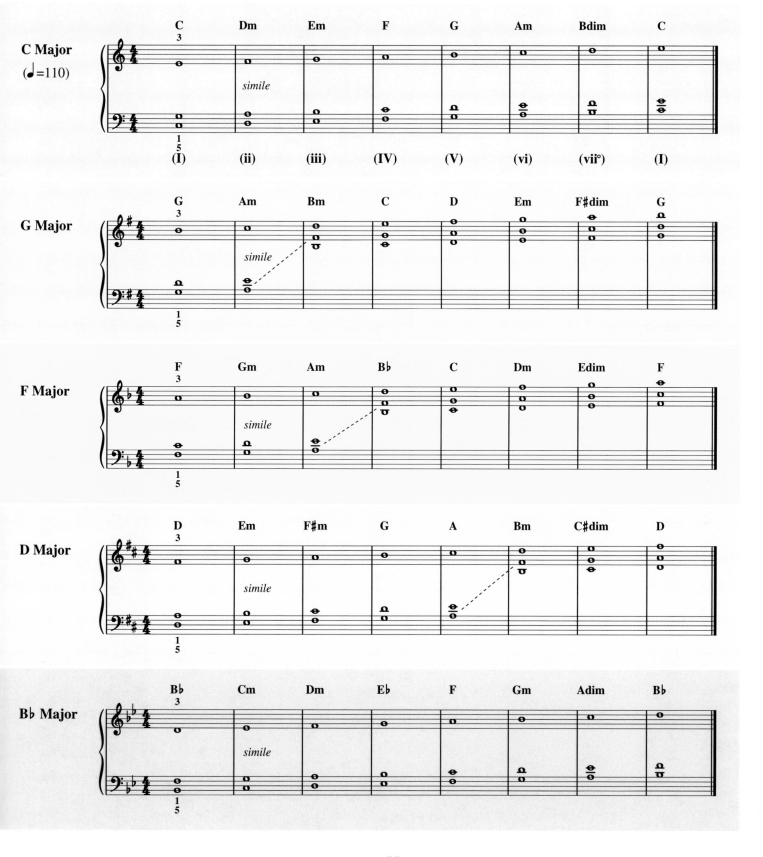

AWARD CERTIFICATE

HAS SUCCESSFULLY COMPLETED
HAL LEONARD PIANO LESSONS,
BOOK FIVE.

TEACHER

DATE

HAL•LEONARD®